Crete: The Graveyard of the Fallschirmjäger

CSC 2005

Subject Area History

===

Crete: The Graveyard of the Fallschirmjäger

SUBMITTED IN PARTIAL FULFILLMENT
OF THE REQUIREMENTS FOR THE DEGREE OF
MASTER OF MILITARY STUDIES

Major George M. Bond, U.S. Army

AY 2004-2005

DISCLAIMER

THE OPINIONS AND CONCLUSIONS EXPRESSED HEREIN ARE THOSE OF
THE INDIVIDUAL STUDENT AUTHOR AND DO NOT NECESSARILY REPRESENT
THE VIEWS OF EITHER THE MARINE CORPS COMMAND AND STAFF COLLEGE
OR ANY OTHER GOVERNMENTAL AGENCY. REFERENCES TO THIS STUDY
SHOULD INCLUDE THE FOREGOING STATEMENT.

Executive Summary

Title: *Crete: The Graveyard of the Fallschirmjager*

Author: **Major George M. Bond, United States Army**

Thesis: The Germans developed an innovative and audacious airborne operational capability, which they employed at the Battle of Crete, but ignored key principles of the offense in order to validate this new concept. By their inability to achieve surprise, concentrate their forces to realize a single purpose, and control the tempo of the attack to retain the initiative, the Germans paratroops were decimated, and only through air superiority and poor Allied leadership were they able to defeat the Allies.

Discussion: On 21 May, 1941 German paratroopers conducted an airborne invasion of the battle of Crete. Rather than being a part of a coherent strategy to defeat the Allies in the Mediterranean, this attack was merely an attempt for Hitler to shore up his southern flank before invading Russia. The author of the airborne plan, General Kurt Student, wanted to prove that airborne troops could be used operationally and drew up the plan to attack Crete with paratroopers and air landed elite mountain troops supported by seaborne reinforcements. Lacking proper resources to conduct the attack and with only three weeks to plan, Student developed a plan to attack the island at four widespread locations. He envisioned complete surprise and failed to make any contingency plans. The Allies defending Crete, having the benefit of intercepted German communications, were prepared for the attack, but lacked the necessary weapons and supplies to properly defend the island. Ten days later the Germans had captured the island, but at a cost of over 6,000 German troops and over 170 transport aircraft.

Conclusion: In Student's rush to prove to the Fuhrer the operational benefit of an airborne force, he ignored key principles of the offense and thus destroyed the very force he advocated. In the end, it was the individual paratrooper that brought Student his victory, but at a terrible cost. Although this Promethean event was an operational and tactical victory for the Germans, it was a Pyrrhic one at best, and Crete would forever be known as the "graveyard of the Fallschirmjäger.

Table of Contents

Page

Disclaimer..i

Executive Summary...ii

Table of Contents..iii

List of Illustrations..iv

List of Tables...v

Introduction...1

Allied Strategy in the Mediterranean..2

Axis Strategy in the Mediterranean..4

Allied Operations in the Mediterranean Theater.....................................9

Axis Operations in the Mediterranean Theater.....................................12

Geography...14

Axis Operational Plans...16

Allied Operational Plans...18

Axis Execution..23

Naval Action...24

The Decisive Point..25

Surprise...27

Concentration..30

Tempo...32

Conclusion..33

Bibliography..35

Illustrations

	Page
Figure 1. Photo of German Paratrooper	1
Figure 2. Relief Map of the Mediterranean	7
Figure 3. Map of the Mediterranean	10
Figure 4. Relief Map of Crete	15
Figure 5. Map of Crete	16
Figure 6. Photo of General Kurt Student	16
Figure 7. Photo of General Alexander Lohr	17
Figure 8. Photo of General Bernard Freyberg	18
Figure 9. Photo of a 40mm Bofors Anit-Aircraft gun	20
Figure 10. Operational Map of Battle of Crete	23
Figure 11. Operational Map of Canae Bay w/ Allied Dispositions	25

Tables

Page

Figure 1. Chain of Command Organizational Table ......………………………......14

Figure 2. Naval Task Force Commanders and Associated Vessels table ……….…..22

THE GERMAN AIRBORNE INVASION OF CRETE: 20 MAY – 01 JUNE 1941

"Of course, General, you know that after Crete we shall never do another Airborne operation ... the day of the Paratroops is over."[1]
--Adolph Hitler

On 20 May 1941, 13,000 German Fallschirmjäger (airborne) soldiers and 9,000 Gebirgsjäger (mountain) troops executed the first strategic airborne operation of World War II by invading the island of Crete. It would also be the last airborne operation for the Axis powers. Facing them were almost 42,000 British, Australian, New Zealand, Greek, and Cretan soldiers and militia. When the smoke cleared a week later, Crete was in the hands of the Germans, but at a horrific cost. Over 6,000 paratroops were killed and the island was littered with 170 transport aircraft and dozens of fighters and bombers shot down by the Allies.[3] The Germans had developed an innovative and audacious airborne operational

---

[1] Maurice Tugwell, A*irborne to Battle: A History of Airborne Warfare 1918-1971* (London, Kimber, 1971), 1.
[2] Postcard reproduction of a painting depicting the jump over Crete on 20.May 1941. (photograph by H.H.Herold)
[3] Douglas Porch, *The Mediterranean Theater in World War II; The Path to Victory* (New York: Farrar, Straus and Giroux, 2004), 173.

capability, but ignored key principles of the offense in order to validate this new concept. By their inability to achieve surprise, concentrate their forces to realize a single purpose, and control the tempo of the attack to retain the initiative, the Germans paratroops were decimated, and only through air superiority and poor Allied leadership were they able to defeat the Allies. As we shall see, the German force was fortunate in being able to recover from its crippling mistakes and achieve a Pyrrhic victory.

Allied Strategy in the Mediterranean

British strategy during the opening of the war was one of survival until it could mobilize its war effort and its primary ally, the United States. By the summer of 1940, France had signed an armistice with Germany, the British Expeditionary Force had been forced to withdraw from Western Europe at Dunkirk, and the northern half of France and all of Belgium, the Netherlands, and Luxembourg had become German-occupied countries. Germany was attempting to starve the British economically by sinking British merchant ships in the Battle of the Atlantic, defeat the British Royal Air Force in the Battle of Britain in order to set the stage for an invasion of their mainland, and finally bomb civilian targets during the Blitz in order to demoralize the British and compel them to sue for peace.[4] Britain persevered, however, and by the fall had the opportunity to transition to the strategic offensive.

Unable to match tank for tank against the Germans, Britain focused on bringing about a German defeat through other, more indirect methods. These included economic warfare, enforced through a naval blockade, aerial bombing, attacking civilian morale as well as economic targets, and 'setting Europe ablaze' through assistance to resistance groups. Another key strategic objective was the removal of Italy from the Axis, whether by military defeat or by inducing the government to change sides. At the operational level of war, British planners favored a 'peripheral' strategy, attacking outlying areas of the German empire so as to tie down and exhaust enemy resources. This plan would prove to be prescient and would occupy British strategic thought until the Normandy invasion in June 1944.

The Mediterranean theater provided the perfect opportunity to implement the British 'peripheral' strategy for a number of reasons. First, a presence in the Mediterranean was necessary to secure the sea lines of communication to its empire in the Mideast and India. The Mediterranean and the Suez Canal shortened the distance oil and other commodities would need to transverse to supply the British Isles, a country already being choked out by German U-boats in the Atlantic Ocean. Second, the Mediterranean theater provided the opportunity for

---

[4] Earl F. Ziemke, *World War II* [online]. California: Victor Valley College [cited 17 November 2004] Available from World Wide Web: (http://www.emayzine.com/lectures/WWII.html), 2.

Britain to prove its resolve against the Axis powers to its potential allies, primarily the United States. This was important, as support for the British cause in the United States was hardly overwhelming in the summer of 1940. In fact, the controversial decision to support Greece in May 1941 was made with "one eye fixed on the impact it would have on U.S. opinion."[5] Turkey and Yugoslavia were other potential allies in the region that Britain hoped to influence. Third, Churchill wanted to clearly separate himself from the failed appeasement policies of Chamberlain and bolster the morale of the British people who were continuously under bombardment from the Lutwaffe during the Blitz. Fourth, Churchill may have wanted to re-engage in the Mediterranean theater as an attempt to atone for the disaster at Gallipoli during World War I.[6] Last, and probably most important, a defeat in this theater, although costly, would not mean the defeat of the British Empire or an abandonment of the Mediterranean.

Axis Strategy in the Mediterranean

Control of the northern Mediterranean was significant for Germany due to its upcoming invasion of Russia. Events in Western Europe in 1940 and 1941, however, had set the stage for operations in the Balkans, Operation MARITA, and for Operation MERCURY, the airborne invasion of Crete. After the German Luftwaffe's defeat in the Battle of Britain in September of 1940, Hitler

---

[5] Porch, 27.
[6] Porch, xi.

indefinitely postponed Operation SEA LION, the planned invasion of Britain. With a paucity of landing craft and a lack of air superiority, Germany did not have the means to attempt any amphibious operation. However, Hitler believed that Britain also did not have the resources to conduct a cross-channel invasion of France and open a Western front. The British expeditionary force recently evacuated from Dunkirk was so weakened and devoid of equipment that it posed no immediate threat. Thus, believing his left flank to be secure, Hitler turned his eyes eastward to the acquisition of a vast, new empire of "lebensraum" (living space) in Russia.

The German invasion of Russia would be its main effort, and every other operation would be subordinate, including Operations MARITA and MERCURY. In August of 1939, Hitler had deftly negotiated a Russo-German alliance, but it was only with the intent to "divert Russia's expansionist ambitions…where their political and military aspirations clashed with German economic interests."[7] Russia should have known that Germany would eventually invade, as Hitler had espoused it as early as 1924 in his book, *Mein Kampf*,

> If new territory were to be acquired in Europe it must have been mainly at Russia's cost, and once again the new German Empire should have set out on its march along the same road as was formerly trodden by the Teutonic Knights, this time to acquire soil for the German plough by means of the German sword and thus provide the nation with its daily bread.[8]

---

[7] Center for Military History, *The German Campaign in the Balkans (Spring 1941)* (CMH Pub 104-4), 7.
[8] Adolph Hitler, *My Struggle* (London, Hurst & Blackett, ltd., 1933), 123.

There were indications that Stalin knew Hitler intended to attack Russia, including the pre-positioning of war stock on the Russo-German border, but Stalin was surprised at the timing. He thought he had another year to prepare for the invasion, but was surprised when Germany invaded in July of 1941.

Hitler also believed a secondary effect of defeating the Russians would be to bring Britain to the bargaining table to sue for peace, as Germany would now be threatening British positions in India and the Middle East. However, this belief was unsupported by reality. If Churchill had refused to negotiate when the British Isles were directly threatened, what made Hitler think that Churchill would capitulate when its colonies were threatened? Cautioned by his generals to wait until the spring to execute Operation BARBAROSSA in order to avoid fighting a winter campaign, Hitler was amenable to shoring up his southern flank for his march east as long as it did not distract from his main effort.

While Hitler was brooding about the Russia invasion, his generals were proposing a strategy to attack the edges of the British Commonwealth. This would be done through operations against its Mediterranean and Imperial holdings with the objective of dislodging the British from Gibraltar, North Africa, and the Suez Canal. They believed this would bring the British to the bargaining table and force them to sign a peace treaty before the Americans got involved. Hitler was more sanguine, but still felt that he could at least defeat the British in the Mediterranean before the invasion of Russia by occupying Gibraltar. Writing to Mussolini in September of 1940, he stated,

> If we encompass the fall of Gibraltar, we shall bolt the western door of the Mediterranean … By the judicious employment of our air force the Mediterranean should become, in three or four months, the tomb of the British Fleet.[9]

Hitler's objective was more limited than his generals' because of his lack of faith in any Italian ability to defeat the British in North Africa and, once again, his preoccupation with Operation BARBAROSSA.

The point became moot, however, because of the unwillingness of Generalissimo Franco of Spain to allow German use of Spanish soil to launch an attack on Gibraltar. With the start of Operation BARBAROSSA approaching, Hitler realized a decisive defeat of the British could not be attained in time. This in turn forced Hitler to further scale back his objectives in the Mediterranean, but it was ultimately Mussolini and the Italians who were to force Germany to become militarily involved in the Mediterranean theater.

---

[9] Chester Wilmot, *The Struggle for Europe* (London: Collins, 1952), 86.

In October of 1940, Mussolini unilaterally staged an attack on Greece, partially to assuage his hurt feelings over Hitler's lack of trust in his compatriot and partially to prove to the world that Italy was not totally dependent on Germany for its survival. The Greeks had been successfully maintaining a fine line between resisting the Axis powers and not provoking Germany, but after being invading by Italy through Albania, they fought ferociously. Hitler was content to let Italy and Greece fight it out amongst them, but the invasion brought the British into the fight, as they had guaranteed Greek independence in 1939 when Italy had invaded Albania.[10] Hitler was loath to divert any of his ground forces from the imminent eastern front to invade Greece, but he could not have the British in Greece threatening his southern flank and, more particularly, the Romanian oil fields at Ploesti. These oil fields supplied "two-thirds of the special fuel required by the Luftwaffe,"[11] fuel that would be needed for Operation BARBAROSSA. Germany also had other vested interests in the Balkans. Hungary supplied and bauxite, Romania supplied grain as well as oil, and Bulgaria offered strategically placed Black Sea ports from which German U-boats could attack Soviet shipping.

Hitler was also playing a chess game in the Balkans with Russia. In June of 1940, Russia laid claim to two Romanian provinces, Bessarabia and northern Bukovina, and was gaining more influence in Yugoslavia due to a common ethnic

---

[10] Antony Beevor, *Crete: The Battle and the Resistance*. Boulder, Colorado: Westview Press, 1994, 7.
[11] I. McD. G. Stewart, *The Struggle for Crete: 20 May – 1 June 1941* (London: Oxford University Press, 1966), 6.

identity with the Serb. Hitler realized that Russia would exploit any sign of weakness on his part and threaten his plans for the upcoming Russian invasion. Hitler thus completely discarded the objective of dislodging the British from the Mediterranean and pursued a strategy of controlling the Balkans. His purpose was to keep it out of the Russian sphere of influence and expelling the British from Greece in order to protect Germany's southern flank for the invasion of Russia.

Preferring diplomacy to military action when interacting with countries sympathetic to the Axis cause, Germany brought Romania and Hungary into the Axis alliance in November 1940 and Bulgaria in March 1941. Hitler had also concluded an agreement with the Regent of Yugoslavia, Prince Paul, but a successful coup the next day stymied these alliance efforts. Enraged at such defiance and the denial of railways important to attacking Greece, Hitler ordered the invasion of Yugoslavia. German troops swept through Yugoslavia in three weeks and were on the Greek border by March of 1941.

Allied Operations in the Mediterranean Theater

British strongholds in the Mediterranean were limited to three locations, Gibraltar, Malta, and Alexandria. Gibraltar provided the British Royal Navy with unimpeded access into the western Mediterranean, and its loss would have forced British shipping to circumnavigate the horn of Africa and pass through the Suez Canal to support operations in North Africa, a task that would have stretched thin British naval assets. Gibraltar was fairly secure because of Generalissimo

Franco's mistrust of Germany. This was confirmed through British intercepts of German communications in December of 1940, when Hitler was forced to cancel Operation FELIX, the German attack on Gibraltar.

The ancient Egyptian port of Alexandria was the only British harbor large enough to berth its Mediterranean fleet and offered a number of airfields from which the RAF could support operations in the Eastern Mediterranean. This position was threatened by the Italians and the Germans under Rommel on a couple of occasions, but remained in British hands for the duration of the war.

Malta was the last remaining stronghold and the most tenuous, as it was subject to daily air attacks by the Luftwaffe and the Italian Navy. Malta's strategic location provided Britain an air and naval base to support its east-west sea lines of communication, and to interdict Axis sea lines to North Africa.

In March of 1941, Allied prospects in North Africa looked promising. The British defeated the Italians at Beda Fomm and decimated an Italian group five times larger. The Allies were likewise poised to push the Italians out of Libya. Churchill's decision to support Greece militarily, however, diverted forces that General Wavell, Commander of the Mideast, needed to prosecute the war in North Africa. Events in Iraq and Palestine were also distracting Wavell. With his limited resources and expanding responsibilities, Wavell found that Churchill was spreading him too thin without prioritizing objectives. This led to the piece-mealing of forces to satisfy Churchill's directions and was in conflict with the primary offensive in North Africa. With the German victory in Greece, Wavell was anxious to redeploy his forces in Greece to Alexandria. Churchill was adamant, however, that Crete was to be defended, as he felt "the successful defence of Crete is one of the most important factors in the defence of Egypt."[12]

Strategically, this made sense. Possession of Crete would give the British Royal Navy the port of Suda, which would allow them to dominate the Eastern Mediterranean. The three airfields would support bases for fighter coverage of the Royal Navy and provide support for future offensive operations into the Balkans. A victory in Crete would also give the Allied forces a boost in morale, as it would be the first Allied defeat of German forces thus far in the war.

Operationally, however, an Allied occupation of Crete was untenable. The geography of Crete forced both the air and port facilities at Suda Bay to be exposed to German air attacks from Greece proper. The Italian occupation of the

---

[12] Telegram from the Prime Minister of the United Kingdom to the Prime Minister of New Zealand, dtd 3 May 1941. This telegram was sent in response to New Zealand's concern that its troops on Crete were not receiving the necessary logistical support as reported up from General Freyberg.

Dodecanese Islands still placed British shipping at risk in the eastern Mediterranean. Lastly, the ability to attack the distant oil fields at Ploesti, a reason cited by both the Germans and the Allies in their desire for Crete, was suspect. At the time, the only British bomber with a range capable of bombing Ploesti was the four-engine long-range *Wellington*. *Wellington* deployment to Crete would have necessitated significant runway and facility modifications and extensions, a difficult prospect under German pressure. Also, any bombing missions made would have to be without fighter support, as the Allies did not yet have a fighter with the necessary range. The implications of the situation meant that any bombing missions by the *Wellingtons* on Ploesti would be ineffective and suicidal.

Churchill persisted in his desire to defend Crete, largely for political and morale reasons, but also because he saw an opportunity to bloody the nose of the Germans. His ace in the hole was Allied intercepts of German "Ultra" communications. In the spring of 1941, "Ultra" communications had been decoded and revealed the invasion of Crete in great detail. With this information in hand, Churchill felt that British forces could not be defeated and was staunch in his desire to retain control of Crete.

Axis Operations in the Mediterranean Theater

With the swift defeat of Yugoslavia, Hitler turned his military might on the Greeks. Even with token support from the British, Greece fell three weeks later. British and Greek forces were forced again, as at Dunkirk, to evacuate under fire.

With the Balkans and Greece firmly under Axis control, Hitler now had a decision to make. Had Germany attained its operational goal of securing its southern flank for the upcoming invasion of Russia or was it necessary to occupy Crete or Malta? Hitler's High command was divided with the Army and Naval components favoring Malta while the air component favored Crete. Once again, it was the requirement of Operation BARBAROSSA that decided the issue. As Douglas Porch writes, "From Hitler's perspective, the conquest of Malta would not knock Britain out of the war, while the conquest of Crete would free him to attack the USSR."[13] In the end Hitler deferred to Reich Marshall Goering, the commander of the Luftwaffe, after being briefed by General Kurt Student on the ability of parachute troops to defeat the allied forces on Crete. On 25 April 1941, Hitler published Directive No. 28, commanding the German Air Force to occupy the island of Crete (see Appendix 1), but with one stipulation. Hitler included in his instructions that "the transport movements must not lead to any delay in the strategic concentration for BARBAROSSA."[14] As Martin Van Creveld observed, "Far from being part of any coherent strategy, therefore, Merkur [Operation MERCURY] was little more than a sop to Goering, whose air force was destined to play a subordinate role in the coming Russian campaign."[15]

There were other twists. Student believed that he would be put in charge of the operation under Goering, but this would not be so. Although he was in charge

---

[13] Porch, 158-159.
[14] Hitler, Directive No. 28.
[15] Martin Van Creveld, Hitler's Strategy, The Balkan Clue, CUP, Cambridge, 1973, 35.

of all ground troops, which were comprised of his paratroopers and the mountain troops attached to him from the Wehrmacht, he was not given control of the aircraft providing close air support. This was given to the commander of the VIII Air Corps and Student's rival, General von Richthofen. Overall command fell on General Lohr, Commander of the 4th Air Fleet, who was limited in his competence by little operational experience with ground forces.[16] The organizational chart for the operation was thus configured:

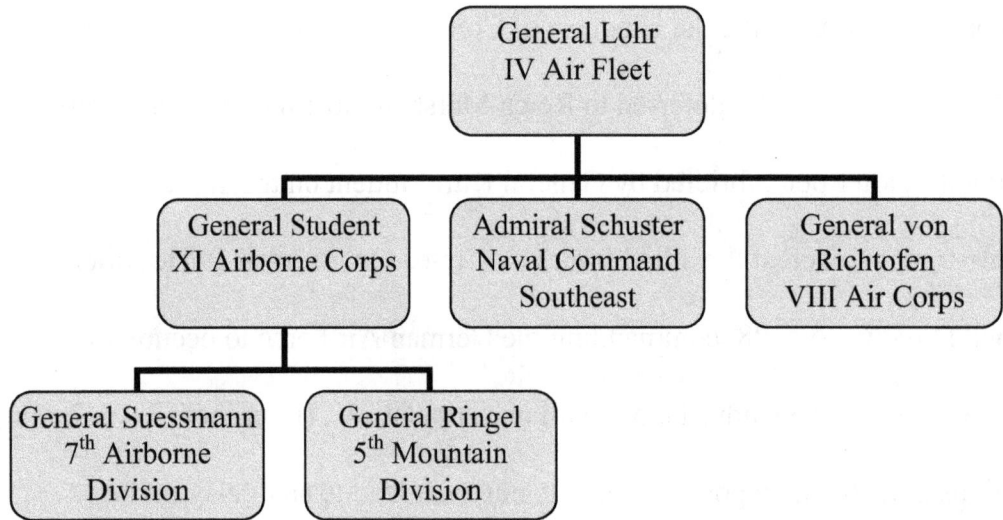

Both Richthofen and Lohr were aware of the impending invasion of Russia and for them this operation was a mere distraction. This attitude and the task organization would cause problems in the prioritization, synchronization, and unity of effort in the upcoming operation.

Geography

Crete, the fifth largest island in the Mediterranean, was positioned at the crossroads of three continents; Europe, Asia and Africa. This mountainous island

---

[16] Department of the Army, German Campaign in the Balkans, 142.

in the eastern Mediterranean is roughly 260 kilometers long and between 20 and 50 kilometers wide. Its north side gently slopes to the sea and offers the only traditional ground line of communication, an east-west road running from Maleme to Heraklion. There are no navigable rivers or north-south lines of communication because of its physical conformation.[17] Crete's geographical position provided a natural defense against enemies attacking from the south, but provided little protection from the north. The German Luftwaffe would maximize this advantage in the upcoming invasion.

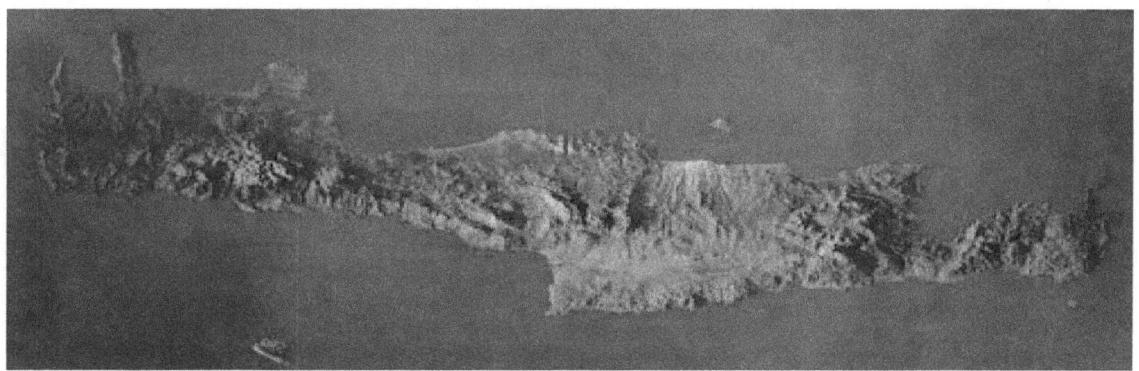

The dock area in the harbor at Suda Bay had been partially destroyed by continued German air. Only two ships at a time could be unloaded, while any others had to remain at anchorage in the bay, prime targets for air attack as the numerous hulks of half-sunken wrecks testified.[18] Key objectives on the island were airstrips

---
[17] Stewart, 34.
[18] Beevor, 66.

located at Maleme, Retimo, and Heraklion.

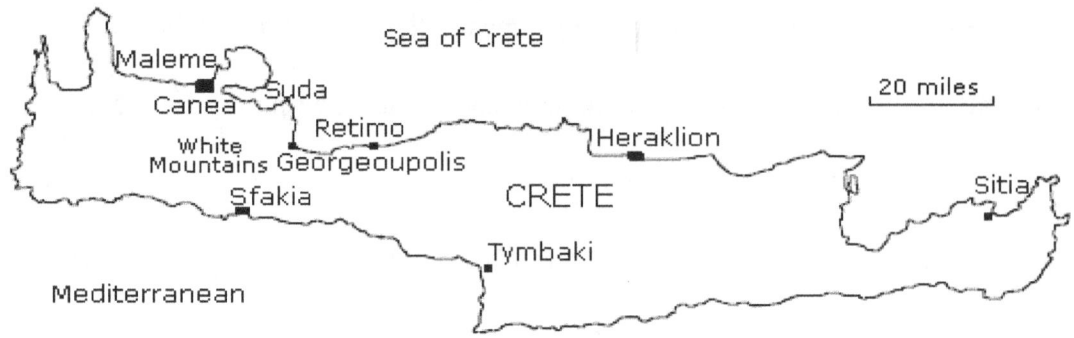

Axis Operational Plans

Initially there were two plans advanced for the invasion of Crete. Student, the German architect of the paratroop division, designed the first plan. An aviator in World War I, Student became enamored with the airborne concept when he witnessed a mass assault of Soviet paratroopers in a 1937 exercise.[19] Soon after, Student stood up the Fliegerkorps XI

and after the highly successful, yet small-scale, airborne assault on the fortress of Eben Emael, became a favorite of Reich Marshall Goering. Student believed that Crete provided the perfect opportunity to validate this new airborne operational concept on a large scale due to Crete's difficult physical geography and the assumption, soon to be proven incorrect, that it would be lightly defended.

Student's plan was to airdrop paratroopers at seven key locations on the island to include primarily Maleme, Canea, Retimo, and Heraklion due to their

---
[19] Porch, 162.

airfields. These airdrops would create a "number of small airheads in the area to be attacked - at first without any definite point of main effort - and then they would expand those airheads with continuous reinforcement until they finally ran together."[20] These expanding "oil spots" would pose multiple dilemmas for the defending Allied forces and would theoretically overwhelm the defense by "putting the Germans in possession of all strategic points on the island in one fell swoop."[21] The lack of developed ground lines of communication would prevent the Allies from deploying reserves or otherwise reinforcing across their entire line of defense.

Lohr, commander of the Air Fleet IV, advanced the other plan. He proposed that there should be one airdrop in the Maleme-Suda sector to concentrate the forces in one location and expand from that location. This would allow both the airborne forces and the supporting airframes to concentrate their firepower in one location. In the end, Herman Goering, Commander-in-Chief of the Luftwaffe,  decided to combine the two plans and planned to airdrop paratroopers into four key locations on the island. Because of the lack of airfields and refueling stations in Greece, the airborne attack would have to split into two sorties: the Maleme-Suda sector would be attacked in the morning, and the Retimo and Heraklion later

---

[20] Center for Military History, *Airborne Operations: A German Appraisal* (CMH Pub 104-13), 5.
[21] CMH Pub 104-4, 126.

in the afternoon. This would be reinforced by a sea invasion west of Maleme on the first day to bring in heavy weapons and the troops of the 5th Mountain division, and another east of Heraklion on the second day.[22] With only three weeks to go before the invasion, preparations for the attack commenced.

Allied Operational Plans

The commander chosen for the defense of Crete was General Bernard Freyberg. Freyberg was born in London but grew up in New Zealand, where he was a  championship swimmer. When war broke out in 1914, Freyberg convinced the then First Lord of the Admiralty Winston Churchill to grant him a commission. Freyberg served gallantly at Gallipoli and on the Western front, and England awarded him the Victoria Cross for actions leading the Royal Naval Division's Hood Battalion in the capture of Beaucourt in Flanders in 1916. He was recalled to active duty upon the outbreak of World War II and was given command of the New Zealand Expeditionary Force largely due to Churchill's intervention. Freyberg's personal heroism during the First World War had engaged Churchill's imagination. As Antony Beevor writes, "Churchill chose men of action, probably because he was a man of action when he was younger. These men of action rarely made good

---

[22] Beevor, 88.

generals."[23] Although Freyberg did not lack personal courage and was beloved by his men as a soldier's soldier, he was probably not the ideal commander to lead the defense of Crete. He lacked the intuition and subtlety to fully understand the operational art of war. He was not known for his intellect, or as General Montgomery put it, "a nice old boy – but a bit stupid."[24] He also yearned for the love of his men rather than their respect, as was evident in his inability to criticize or even fire underperforming subordinates. Lastly, Freyberg was known to be obstinate, refusing to give ground or adjust a plan based on operational necessity.

The decision to appoint Freyberg as the commander of the defense of Crete was born more out of opportunity than of design. Having commanded his troops in the abortive attempt to defend Greece, he had been evacuated to Crete along with half his forces. He assumed that he would subsequently be evacuated to North Africa, link up with the rest of his command, the 2d New Zealand Expeditionary Force, and reconstitute and refit. On 30 April, however, General Wavell visited Crete and personally asked him to command the troops left behind to defend Crete, commonly known as Creforce. Freyberg reluctantly agreed, noting in a dispatch to the New Zealand Minister of Defense that, "I have therefore done so as a temporary measure only."[25] the attitude evidenced in these actions was not one of high commitment. Freyberg clearly was a reluctant player, a bad omen.

---

[23] Beevor, 84.
[24] Nigel Hamilton, *Master of the Battlefield: Monty's War Years, 1942-1944* (New York: McGraw Hill, 1983), 238.
[25] Dispatch 389.

The situation in which Freyberg found himself seemed, at first glance, to be pretty bleak. The island garrison consisted of about 27,500 British and imperial troops and 14,000 Greeks. Of these, 5,000 had been the original garrison and were fairly well equipped, while the rest were evacuees from Greece. These soldiers were tired, disorganized and ill equipped with only the light weapons that could be personally carried during a rushed evacuation.[26] The force had only five anti-aircraft batteries, the QF 40-mm Anti-Aircraft Gun (The Bofors), hardly a defense against an airborne attack. There was also 45 pieces of artillery that had largely been from the Italians and six infantry tanks.[27] The Allied air support might have consisted of six Hurricanes, but these were removed from the island a few days before the German attack. The only plane in the British inventory that could support Crete was a Hurricane equipped with a drop tank for the 350-mile flight from Alexandria. This meant that the planes could only make brief appearances over the battlefield.[28]

Given these scarce resources, Freyberg was presented with two clear choices in defense of the island. The first was to disperse his forces in order to protect both the aerodromes against an airborne attack and the beaches in the

---

[26] Peter Deniston and Patrick Kiser, "Operation Merkur: Invasion of Kreta," 2001. <Gebirgsjaeger.4mg.com/kreta.htm>
[27] D. M. Davin, "Crete," *Official History of New Zealand in the Second World War 1939–45,* 2004. <Nzetc.org/etexts/WH2-1D/c18.html>
[28] Porch, 168.

vicinity against a supporting seaborne attack. The second was to concentrate his forces in four self-contained groups for the immediate defense of the three aerodromes and the base area of Suda and to accept risk in not defending against a sea borne assault. Freyberg chose the first option, in part because of his cautious nature and the intelligence being fed to him from London and ULTRA intercepts.

On April 25, Bletchey Park, the British signals intelligence section, intercepted and deciphered Hitler's original Directive No. 28.[29] The Germans had been forced to use radio signals to broadcast the plan in detail due to their compressed timetable for the operation and the dispersed nature of the troops that were to mount it. This intelligence was then fed to Freyberg, but it was sanitized to protect the source of the intelligence. It was this sanitization that caused Freyberg to believe the main effort of the attack was to be an air drop at Heraklion accompanied by a seaborne assault. After the war, Freyberg admitted to Churchill "we, for our part, were mostly preoccupied by sea-landings, not by the threat of air-landings."[30]

While Freyberg was the ground commander, Admiral Andrew Cunningham, Commander-in-Chief, Mediterranean, was in charge of the naval forces. He organized his task force as follows:

---

[29] Ronald Lewin, *Ultra goes to War*, (NY: McGraw Hill Book co., 1978), 15.
[30] Davin Papers, Freyberg comments on Churchill Draft, 3 March 1949.

UNIT	COMMANDER	SHIPS
Force A1	Admiral H. Rawlings	Battleships - *Warspite, Valiant*
Force B		Cruisers - *Gloucester, Fiji*
Force C	Admiral E. L. S. King	Cruisers - *Naiad, Perth* Destroyers - *Kandahar, Nubian, Kingston, Juno* AA Cruiser - *Calcutta*
Force D	Admiral I. G. Glennie	Cruisers - *Dido, Orion, Ajax* Destroyers - *Napier, Kimberley, Isis, Janus, Griffin, Imperial*
Force E	Captain P. J. Mack	Destroyers - *Jervis, Nizam, Ilex* AA Cruiser - *Carlisle*

These naval forces found themselves in the unenviable position of having no air defense from land-based air forces and the only aircraft carrier in the Eastern Mediterranean, *Formidable*, conducting convoy security in the area and down to only four serviceable aircraft.[31] The mission of this naval force was to prevent the Germans from conducting a seaborne landing on the coast of Crete. As the *London Gazette* published in its well-known account of the battle, "It was known that airborne invasion of the island was impending; but it appeared almost

---

[31] John Dillon, "The Battle of Crete," *Naval Action against the German Flotillas*, 2003. <Home.freeuk.net/johndillon/sea_invasion.htm>

inconceivable that airborne invasion alone could succeed against forewarned troops, that seaborne support was inevitable and that the destruction of troop convoys would win the day."[32]

Axis Execution

The invasion of Crete began at 0800 on the morning of May 20 with airdrops at Maleme and Canea. Losses were initially heavy, as German intelligence had underestimated the number of Allied troops defending Crete by some 35,000 men. German intelligence had also failed to realize that a larger number of Allied troops had evacuated to Crete and not to Alexandria. Also, due to the design of the German parachute, the Germans could not jump with anything larger than a pistol. Those who were not killed in the air were shot on the ground, as they searched for their heavy weapons. These had been simultaneously dropped with an identifying color parachute, but as in all such operations, men and weapons were never close together.

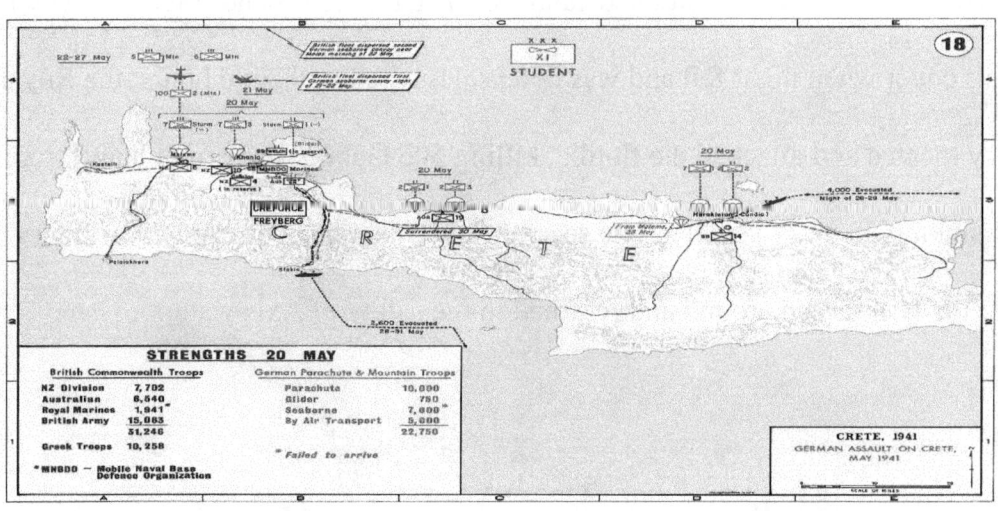

---

[32] Supplement to the London Gazette, 21 May 1948, 1.

By midday, the Germans had failed to secure their objectives in the Maleme-Suda sector. Their superior discipline and training and Luftwaffe close air support preserved the force.

The airdrops scheduled for Retimo and Heraklion met with even worse disaster. Due to refueling delays and high winds at the originating airfields, the drops in the west were staggered and uncoordinated with close air support. This mistiming resulted in even greater casualties than in the west. Once again German intelligence had failed the paratroops by estimating 400 Allied troops at Heraklion and none at Retimo.[33]

Naval Action

The biggest disaster would be suffered by the seaborne reinforcement. A flotilla of 63 requisitioned vessels departed the island of Milos under the cover of the Luftwaffe. The flotilla was delayed due to poor weather and the suspect seaworthiness of the requisitioned caiques. The makeshift and fragile convoy lost its air cover when night fell and was defenseless. Around 2300 hours, the Royal Navy located and attacked the flotilla, killing 506 Gebirgsjäger (mountain) troops and sinking 20 of 21 vessels. The second flotilla that had departed a few hours after the first turned around and returned to the safety of Axis waters. There

---

[33] Beevor, 79.

would be no more attempts to reinforce Crete from the sea until the island was secured.[34]

Subsequent naval action, however, was severely reduced, as land-based German aircraft pounded the Royal Navy and sunk over nine ships in a force of 24. The belief that naval anti-aircraft weapon systems alone were sufficient to defend against air attack was false, and Cunningham realized that in this instance without the air cover afforded by a carrier air wing, "control of the sea had passed from surface forces to air power."[35]

The Decisive Point

The decisive terrain in the operation was Hill 107, occupied by the 22nd New Zealand battalion, overlooking the Maleme airfield. From this position, the Kiwis were able to attack the field by direct fire and prevent the Germans from

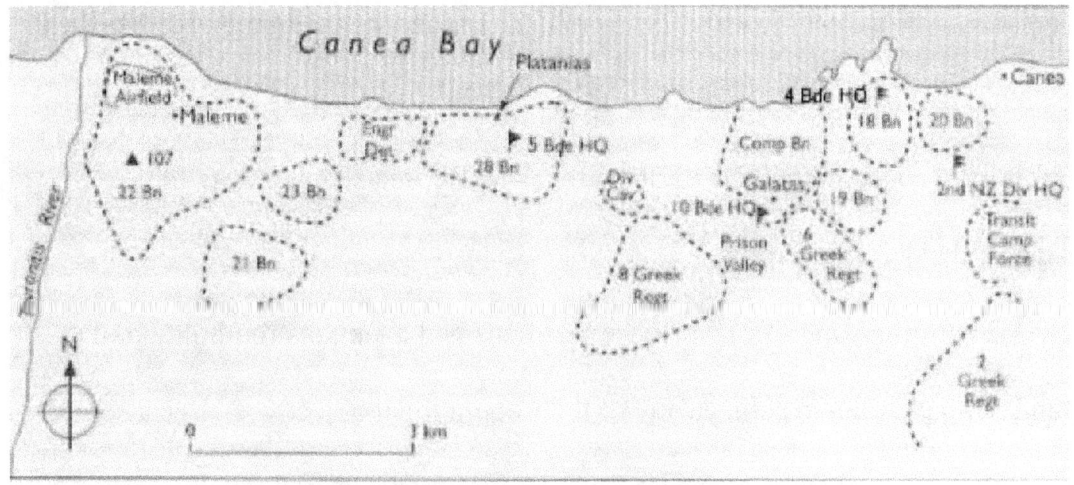

---

[34] CMH Pub 104-4, 133.
[35] Kelly Bell, "Costly Capture of Crete," *World War II*. May 1999, 2.

landing reinforcements. On the night of 20 May, the Commander of the 22nd New Zealand Battalion, Lieutenant-Colonel L.W. Andrew, feeling pressure from pockets of German paratroopers, withdrew from this dominating position. This gave the Germans the opportunity to occupy it the next morning unopposed and thus to secure their position. While many blame this withdrawal on Andrew's loss of nerve, there were others to blame for this tactical blunder. The commanders of the neighboring 21st and 23rd battalions had been given orders to counterattack, if the Germans had "secured a lodgment on the airfield."[36] This they did not do. The brigade commander, Brigadier James Hargest, has come under fire for so easily acquiescing to the request by Andrew to pull back by responding, "if you must, you must." This was communicated to his subordinates from his headquarters well to the rear and well beyond his ability to effectively command and control his brigade. Lastly, Freyberg himself has been blamed for overestimating the enemy's ability to conduct a seaborne landing on the beaches of Crete. By covering the airfields and the beaches, Freyberg's troops were too dispersed to concentrate their combat power on the decisive point, or in this instance, the decisive terrain.

By the morning of 21 May, the Germans had a tenuous foothold on the island but had failed to achieve any of their operational objectives. Because of Student's overconfidence of success in his initial drops, he had failed to plan for

---

[36] Ian McGibbon, "Battle for Crete: The Controversies," Wellington, N.Z.: Ministry for Culture and Heritage, (www.nzhistory.net.nz/Gallery/crete/controversies.htm).

an operational reserve to reinforce success or shore up difficulties. The confusion caused by the refueling delay of the second wave, however, had stranded a battalion of paratroops, which he quickly reorganized into his reserve force. Although communications with the ground troops on Crete was practically non-existent, Student recognized that his only opportunity to turn the tide of battle would be to reinforce the Maleme-Suda sector. He consequently dropped his reserves at the Maleme airfield and, with Andrew's unexpected withdrawal from the high ground, was able to expand his perimeter. This permitted follow-on troops to be landed at Maleme and reinforce his ground forces. This tipped the balance in the favor of the Germans, and on 1 June, British forces surrendered, leaving 17,000 men to be taken prisoner. The Germans themselves lost 7,000 troops in their victory.[37]

Surprise

In the offense, commanders achieve surprise by attacking the enemy at a time or place he does not expect or in a manner for which he is unprepared ... Surprise delays enemy reactions, overloads and confuses his command and control (C2) systems, induces psychological shock in enemy soldiers and leaders, and reduces the coherence of the defense.[38]

According to MCDP 1-3, surprise can be achieved through "deception, stealth, and ambiguity," and "can often prove decisive,"[39] yet the Germans did not achieve surprise at the operational or tactical level of war.

---

[37] John Rickard, *Operation Mercury: The German Invasion of Crete, 20 May – 1 June 1941* (London: Hodder and Stoughton, 2002), 12.
[38] Department of the Army, *Operations*, FM 3-0 (Washington, DC: 14 June 2001), 7-4
[39] MCDP 1-3, Tactics, 30 July 1997, 47.

Neither Lohr nor Student made any attempt to execute an operational or tactical deception plan. North Africa and the island of Malta were alternative operational targets to Crete and could have been used. Had an attempt been made to put doubt in the Allies mind, the Germans might have forced the diversion of a portion of the British Fleet to cover these other targets. This would have been significant in the first two days of the battle, as the British Fleet was able to prevent the seaborne reinforcements. Student also developed no tactical deception plan. The development of false drop zones and use of the Luftwaffe to deflect attention from the primary objectives could have bought the paratroopers the necessary few minutes needed to land, collect their heavy weapons, and form into capable fighting units.

Due to the condensed timetable for the attack caused by the upcoming invasion of Russia, Student was unable to practice good operations security. German activity in preparation for the attack gave the Allies numerous sources of information to analyze. Airfields for the transport aircraft had to be cobbled out of the countryside as the Luftwaffe's fighters and bombers had taken possession of the fixed and improved airfields that already existed in southern Greece. Paratroopers scattered throughout Western Europe had to be recalled and pre-positioned. Over 300 aircraft had to be sent to Germany for quick repairs and then flown back to southern Greece. The British collected all these indicators as they continuously flew reconnaissance aircraft over southern Greece. The Germans made no attempt to deny the enemy information regarding their preparations, and this lack of stealth should have been recognized by Student and accounted for in a deception plan. The Allies clearly were aware of an impending attack and from where it was coming. Student, however, could have deceived them as to where the attack was going to be.

Finally, there was no plan to exploit the built-in ambiguity of Student's plan. The Germans were no strangers to ambiguity as "ambiguity was central to the tactics of the World War II German blitzkrieg."[40] The use of several drop zones to attack the island led the Allies to spread their forces thinly, as they could not identify the main effort. However, Student's plan lacked the necessary reinforcements to accommodate setbacks and overcome them. The ambiguousness of Student's plan turned out to be successful, as Freyberg still believed on day three that the main effort was Heraklion.

The one wild card in the deck, and one that Student could not have known about, was that the British through the Ultra intercepts were deciphering German communications about the operation. These intercepts revealed the entire German battle strategy to include situation reports, reinforcement rates, and the actual identification of units landing on Crete.[41] Luckily for the Germans, the Allies incorrectly analyzed some of this intelligence and over-sanitized it so that Freyberg was confused and divided his forces to interdict what he thought would be a simultaneous air and sea invasion.

---

[40] MCDP 1-3, 49.
[41] F. H. Hinsley, *British Intelligence during the Second World War*, (London: Majesty's Stationary Office [HMSO], 1979), p. 420.

Concentration

Concentration is the massing of overwhelming effects of combat power to achieve a single purpose. By massing forces rapidly along converging axes, attackers overwhelm enemy forces at decisive points with concentrated combat power. After a successful attack, commanders keep their forces concentrated to take advantage of their momentum.[42]

By dropping onto four different objectives split into two sorties, the German paratroops failed to mass any combat power on their objectives. This was partially due to the Germans grossly underestimating the Allied forces defending the island, particularly at the airfields. The initial airdrops were designed to shock and overwhelm the airfield defenders but instead the defenders turned them into kill zones of concentrated fire. Those Germans not killed in the air were killed on the ground while they searched for their crew-served and heavy weapons. Ironically, the only paratroops that were able to mass together were those that were incorrectly placed outside the planned drop zones away from the airfields.

As the first sortie returned to the originating airfields to refuel, Student had an opportunity to revise his drop plan and send troops to the Maleme-Suda sector to mass his combat power. He was unaware, however, of the events taking place on Crete, because his communication support had been stripped for the invasion of Russia. Without any operational awareness, Student sent the second sortie on to Retimo and Heraklion, where his men would suffer the same fate as those in the first sortie.

---

[42] Department of the Army, FM 3-0, 7-5.

The four objectives chosen for the drops were miles apart and could not mutually support each other. After the initial attack, it could only be through the capture of the airfields that airborne reinforcements could be brought in, expand the position, and link up with the adjoining troops to mass their combat power. General Student made a false assumption that all four objectives would be captured quickly to allow for follow-on forces to be flown in. It was to be a friction-less fight. Student's only allowance for the possibility that none of the airfields would be seized the first day was to have the seaborne reinforcements to arrive the first and second days. Yet, the seaborne movement plan was more of an afterthought and was incomplete. The Germans lacked adequate naval transport for their troops and could not protect their amphibious operation. The commander of the 5th Mountain Division, General Julius Ringel, observed "the only navigational equipment available for the naval expedition had consisted of a 1/500,000 map and a pocket compass."[43]

Concentration, or focus as described in MCDP 1, also "applies to time as well as space," and one "must focus effects not only at the decisive location but also at the decisive moment."[44] This lack of focus was demonstrated by the failure to integrate airdrops and coordinated air support for a number of reasons. First, with Hitler's emphasis on Operation BARBAROSSA, the Crete invasion was not allocated sufficient air support. Second, the command structure was such that the

---

[43] Henry Harmeling, Armor vs. Paratroopers, U.S. Army Combat Force Journal, Vol IV, No. 7, 1954, 24.
[44] MCDP 1, 41.

ground commander, Student, did not have any control over his close air support and could not adjust its application during the operation. Third, Student had been overly optimistic about the successful timing of the attacks and had not allowed himself any flexibility to account for friction. Nowhere was this more evident than in the execution of the second sortie of paratroopers destined for Heraklion and Retimo. Conditions at the launching airfields were so dusty that the aircraft had to wait ten minutes between take-offs to let the dust clear for safe visibility. This condition was exacerbated by the aircraft refueling that had to be done by hand pump, and that caused the staggered departures of transport aircraft, fighters and bombers for the airdrop. This forced the paratroopers to jump into the fight only 20 at a time and up to thirty minutes apart.[45] Fighter and bomber support was likewise affected and became random and uncoordinated.

Tempo

Controlling or altering tempo is necessary to retain the initiative. At the operational level, a faster tempo allows attackers to disrupt enemy defensive plans by achieving results quicker than the enemy can respond ... By increasing tempo, commanders maintain momentum ... While maintaining a tempo faster than the enemy's, attackers balance the tempo with the ability to exercise C2 ... Commanders never permit the enemy to recover from the shock of the initial assault. They prevent defenders from massing effects against the friendly decisive operation.[46]

With the total lack of surprise and the inability to mass effective combat power on objectives, Student had lost control over the tempo of the operation. The lack of

---

[45] Stewart, 201.
[46] Department of the Army, 7-6.

adequate intelligence or communication with his troops on the first day of the attack prevented him from making proper decisions to improve the tempo and regain the initiative. Even if he had been able to do this, he had not planned on an operational reserve to reinforce success or to counterattack failure. When the British fleet destroyed his seaborne reinforcements, it was only through serendipity that he had a battalion of paratroops left behind from the second sortie. When the Allies inexplicably retreated from the high ground controlling the Maleme airfield, Student regained the initiative by air-landing those troops to secure Maleme. With the influx of reinforcements, Student was able to increase the tempo of the operation, mass his combat forces, and eventually overcome the Allies.

Conclusion

General Student had predicated his plan on a number of faulty assumptions and had failed to make any contingency plans. In his rush to prove to the Fuhrer the operational benefit of an airborne force, he ignored key principles of the offense and thus destroyed the very force he advocated. In the end, it was the individual paratrooper that brought Student his victory, but at a terrible cost. Hitler never used an airborne attack again, instead splitting up the XI Airborne Corps and using them as an elite ground force. Ironically, it would be the Allies who would benefit from this operation and successfully conduct airborne operations in Italy, France, and Belgium. Although this Promethean event was an operational and tactical victory for the Germans, it was a Pyrrhic one at best, and Crete would forever be known as the "graveyard of the Fallschirmjäger."

Bibliography

Beevor, Antony. *Crete: The Battle and the Resistance*. Boulder, Colorado: Westview Press, 1994.

Bell, Kelly. "Costly Capture of Crete." *World War II*. May 1999.

Churchill, Winston S. *The Grand Alliance*. Cambridge: The Riverside Press, 1950.

Cunningham, Admiral Sir Andrew B. "The Battle of Crete" published as a supplement to The *London Gazette*. 21 May 1948.

Davin, D. M. "Crete" *Official History of New Zealand in the Second World War 1939–45,* 2004. (http://www.Nzetc.org/etexts/WH2-1D/c18.html).

Deniston, Peter and Patrick Kiser. "Operation Merkur: Invasion of Kreta," 2001. (http://www.Gebirgsjaeger.4mg.com/kreta.htm).

Department of the Army, *Operations*, FM 3-0. Washington, DC: 14 June 2001.

Dillon, John. "The Battle of Crete." *Naval Action against the German Flotillas*, 2003. (http://www.Home.freeuk.net/johndillon/sea_invasion.htm).

Hamilton, Nigel. *Master of the Battlefield: Monty's War Years, 1942-1944*. New York: McGraw Hill, 1983.

Harmeling, Henry, "Armor vs. Paratroopers." *U.S. Army Combat Force Journal*. Vol IV, No. 7, 1954.

Hinsley, F. H. *British Intelligence during the Second World War*. London: Majesty's Stationary Office [HMSO], 1979.

Hitler, Adolph. *My Struggle*. London: Hurst & Blackett, ltd., 1933.

Lewin, Ronald. *Ultra Goes to War*. New York: McGraw Hill Book Co., 1978.

Marine Corps Doctrinal Publication. *Tactics*. MCDP 1-3. Washington, DC: 30 July 1997.

McGibbon, Ian. "Battle for Crete: The Controversies." Wellington, N.Z.: Ministry for Culture and Heritage. (www.nzhistory.net.nz/Gallery/crete/controversies.htm)

Porch, Douglas. *The Mediterranean Theater in World War II; The Path to Victory*. New York: Farrar, Straus and Giroux, 2004.

Rickard, John. *Operation Mercury: The German Invasion of Crete, 20 May – 1 June 1941*. London: Hodder and Stoughton, 2002.

Stewart, I. McD. G. *The Struggle for Crete: 20 May – 1 June 1941*. London: Oxford University Press, 1966.

Tugwell, Maurice. *Airborne to Battle: A History of Airborne Warfare 1918-1971*. London: Kimber, 1971.

U.S. Army Center for Military History, *The German Campaign in the Balkans (Spring 1941)*. CMH Pub 104-4. Washington D.C.: U.S. Government Printing Office, 1984.

U.S. Army Center for Military History, *Airborne Operations: A German Appraisal*. CMH Pub 104-13. Washington D.C.: U.S. Government Printing Office, 1989.

Van Creveld, Martin. *Hitler's Strategy, The Balkan Clue*. Cambridge: Cambridge University Press, 1973.

Wilmot, Chester. *The Struggle for Europe*. London: Collins, 1952.

Ziemke, Earl F. "World War II". (http://www.emayzine.com/lectures/WWII.html).

www.ingramcontent.com/pod-product-compliance
Lightning Source LLC
Chambersburg PA
CBHW081300170426
43198CB00017B/2860